1. In the Name of the Lord
(1 Samuel 16:1-1 Samuel 18:9)

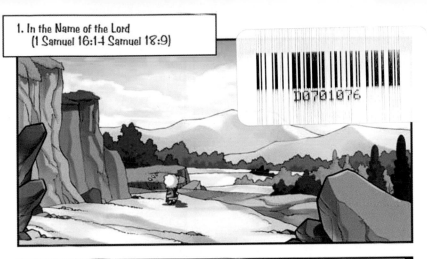

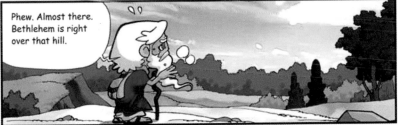

Phew. Almost there. Bethlehem is right over that hill.

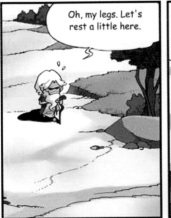

Oh, my legs. Let's rest a little here.

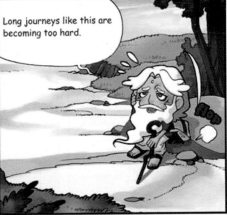

Long journeys like this are becoming too hard.

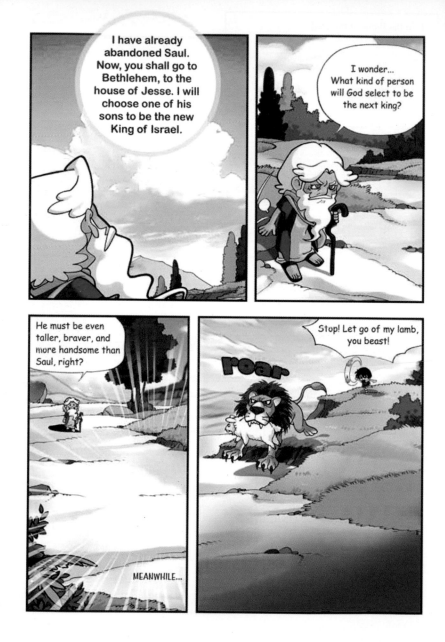

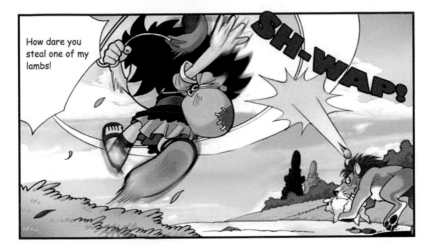

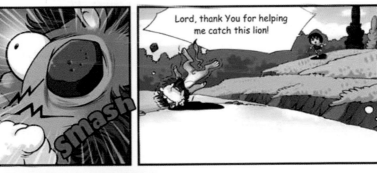

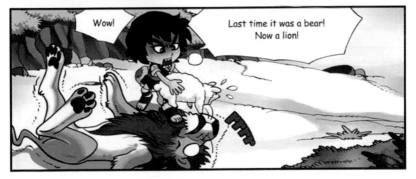

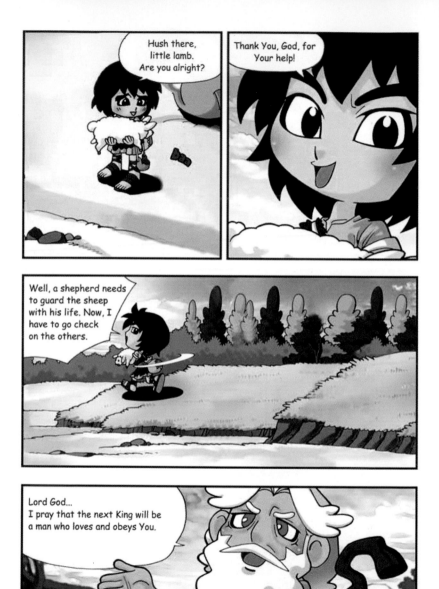

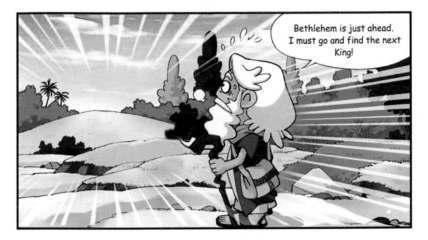

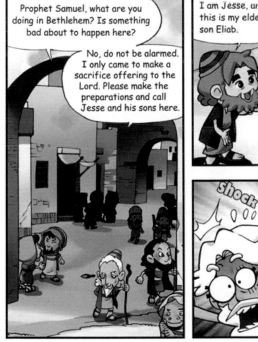

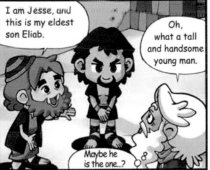

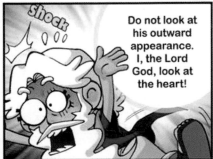

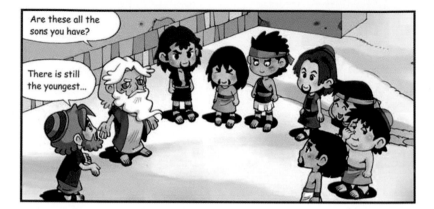

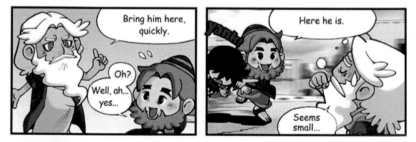

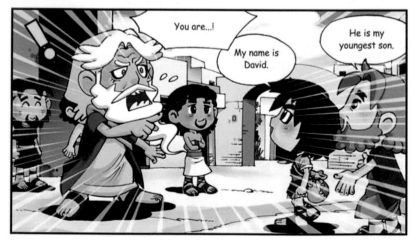

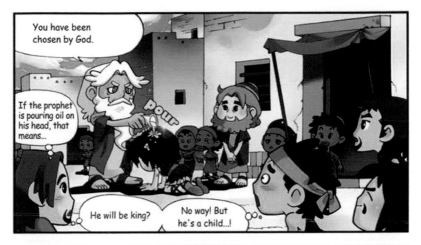

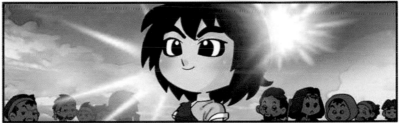

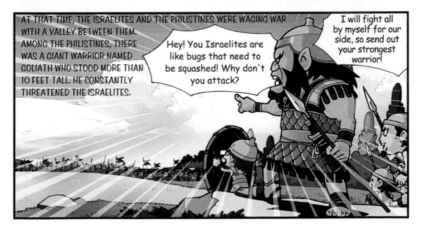

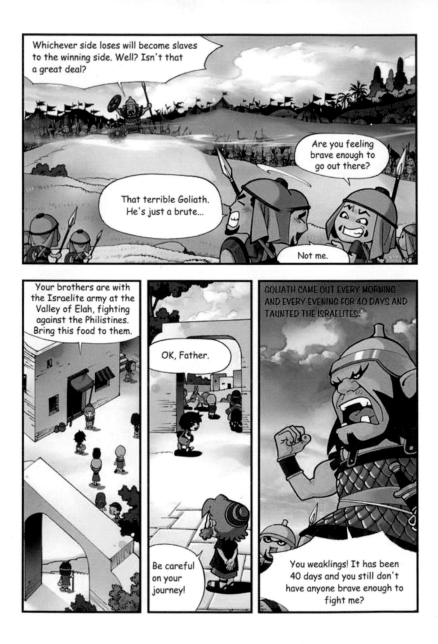

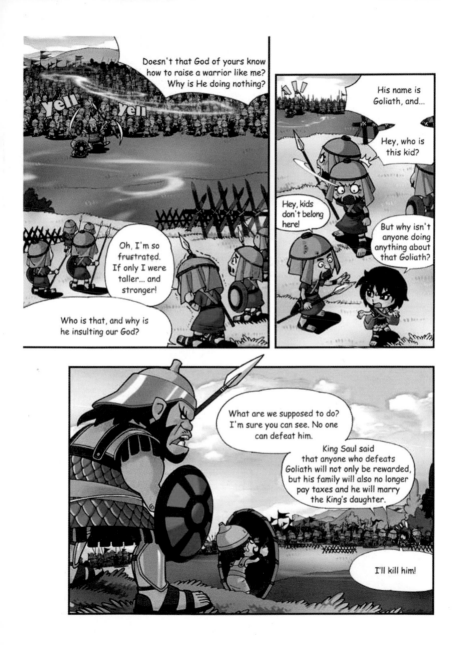

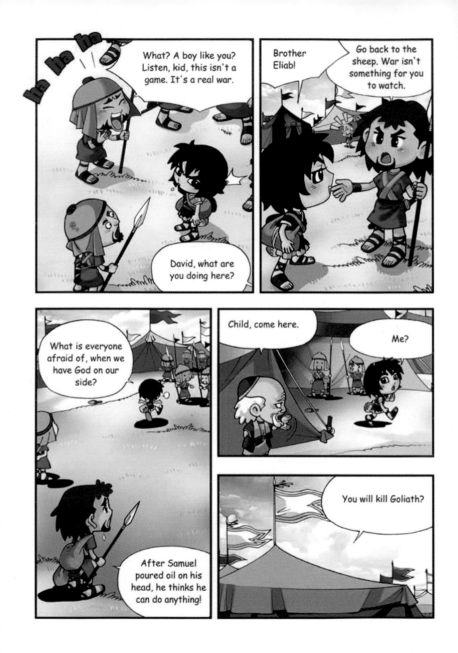

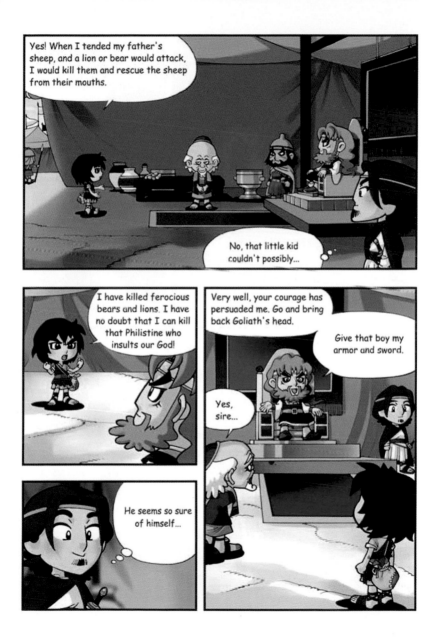

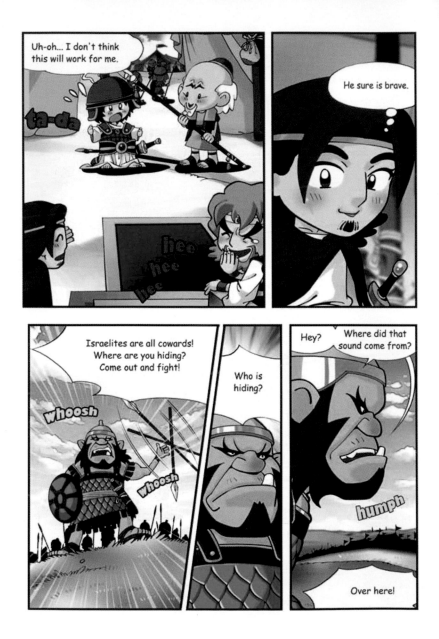

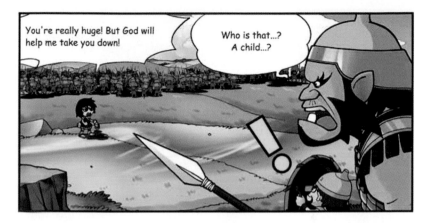

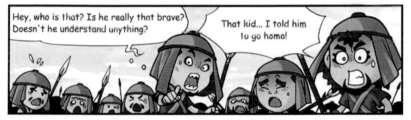

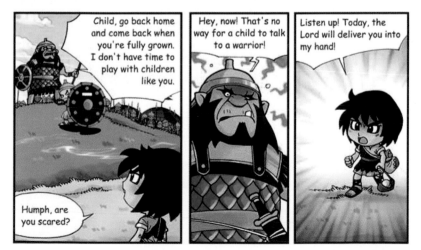

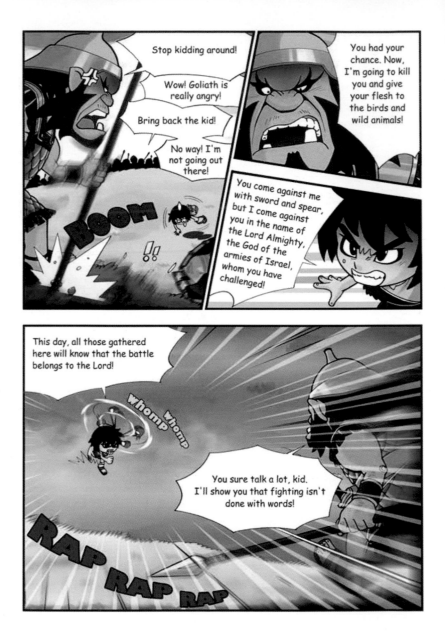

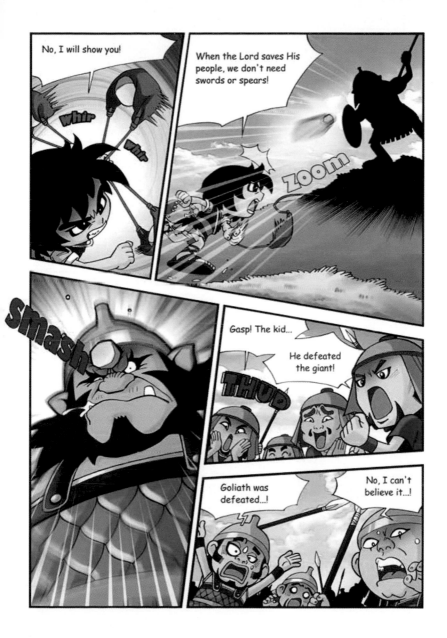

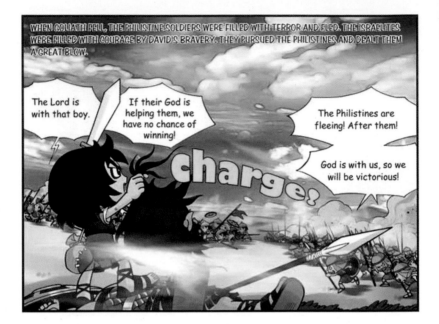

Find out more about David in

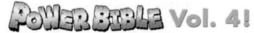 **Vol. 4!**

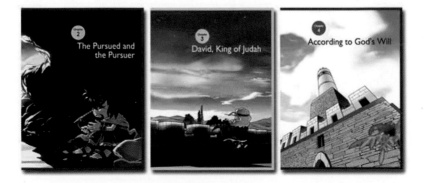